THE KIDS' BOOK OF FUN FOR THE ROAD

By The Diagram Group

TREASURE PRESS

Thls book has lots of things to look out for on a long car journey. You should be able to enjoy finding them as you travel along, or perhaps when you stop for petrol or for something to eat. Why not keep a log book of your journey and make a note of when and where you spot all the things mentioned in this book?

While you are trying to answer the questions put your hand over the answers.

First published in Great Britain in 1977 by
Sidgwick and Jackson Limited under the title
The Junior Book of the Road

This edition published in 1986 by
Treasure Press
59 Grosvenor Street
London W1

Copyright 1977 by Diagram Visual Information Limited

ISBN 1 85051 106 3

Printed in Portugal by Oficinas Gráficas ASA

Reprinted 1987

Watch out!

How many of these things can you spot on your journey today?

Den Dolder 4
Zeist 1 Utrecht 14

50

COVER ILLUSTRATION: GRAHAM THOMPSON

Contents

Nottingham
A 52
1⁄2m

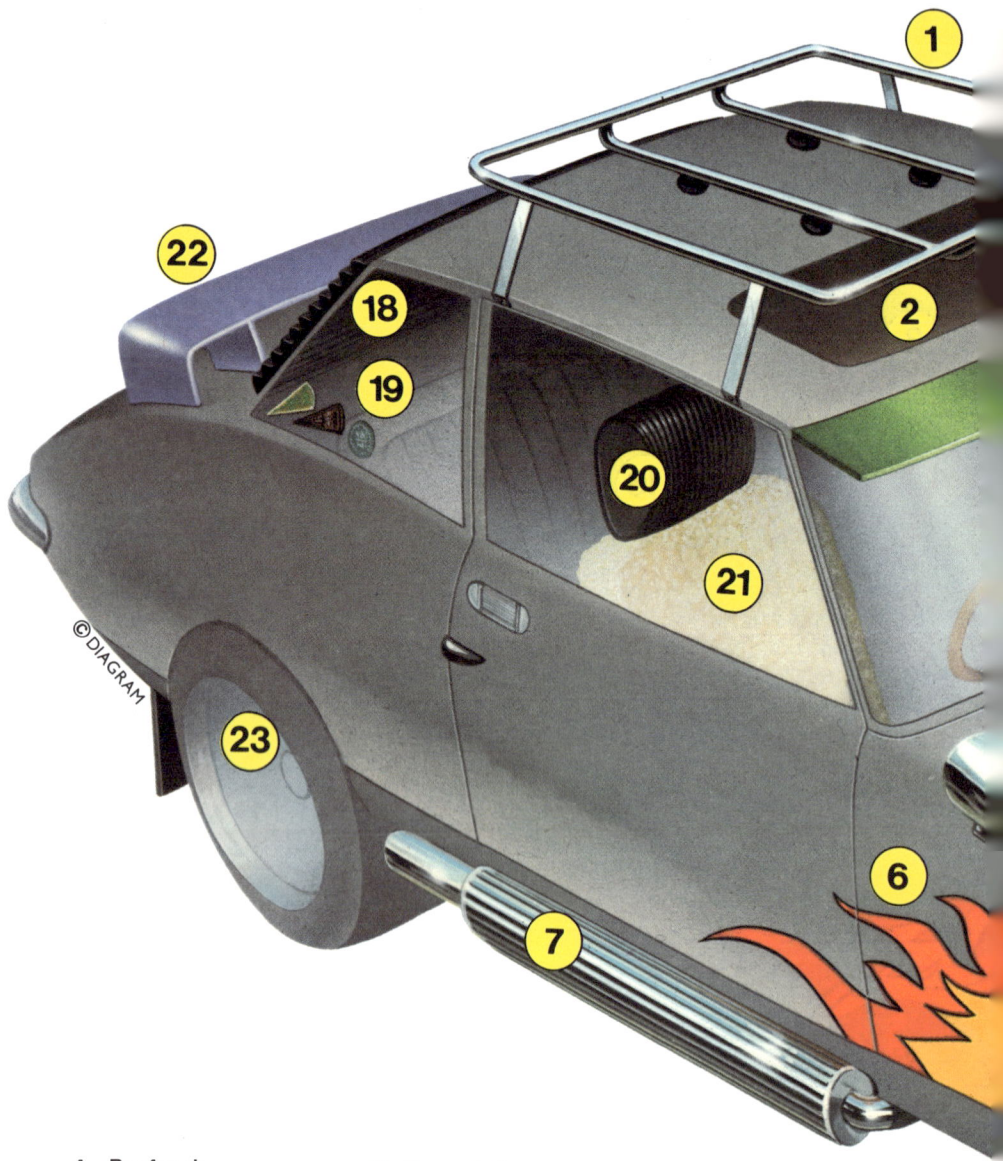

1	Roof rack	**9**	Snowchains	**17**	Aerial
2	Sliding roof	**10**	Fog lamps	**18**	Louvred window
3	Visor	**11**	Club badges	**19**	Holiday stickers
4	Wood steering wheel	**12**	Maker's badge	**20**	Head restraint
5	Driving mirror	**13**	Spot lamp cover	**21**	Seat cover
6	"Customized" painting	**14**	Road fund licence	**22**	Aerofoil
7	Exterior exhaust	**15**	Parking permit	**23**	Wide wheels
8	Mud flaps	**16**	Wiper aerofoils		

The personal touch

**How many of these things
can you find on your car,
or on other people's cars?**

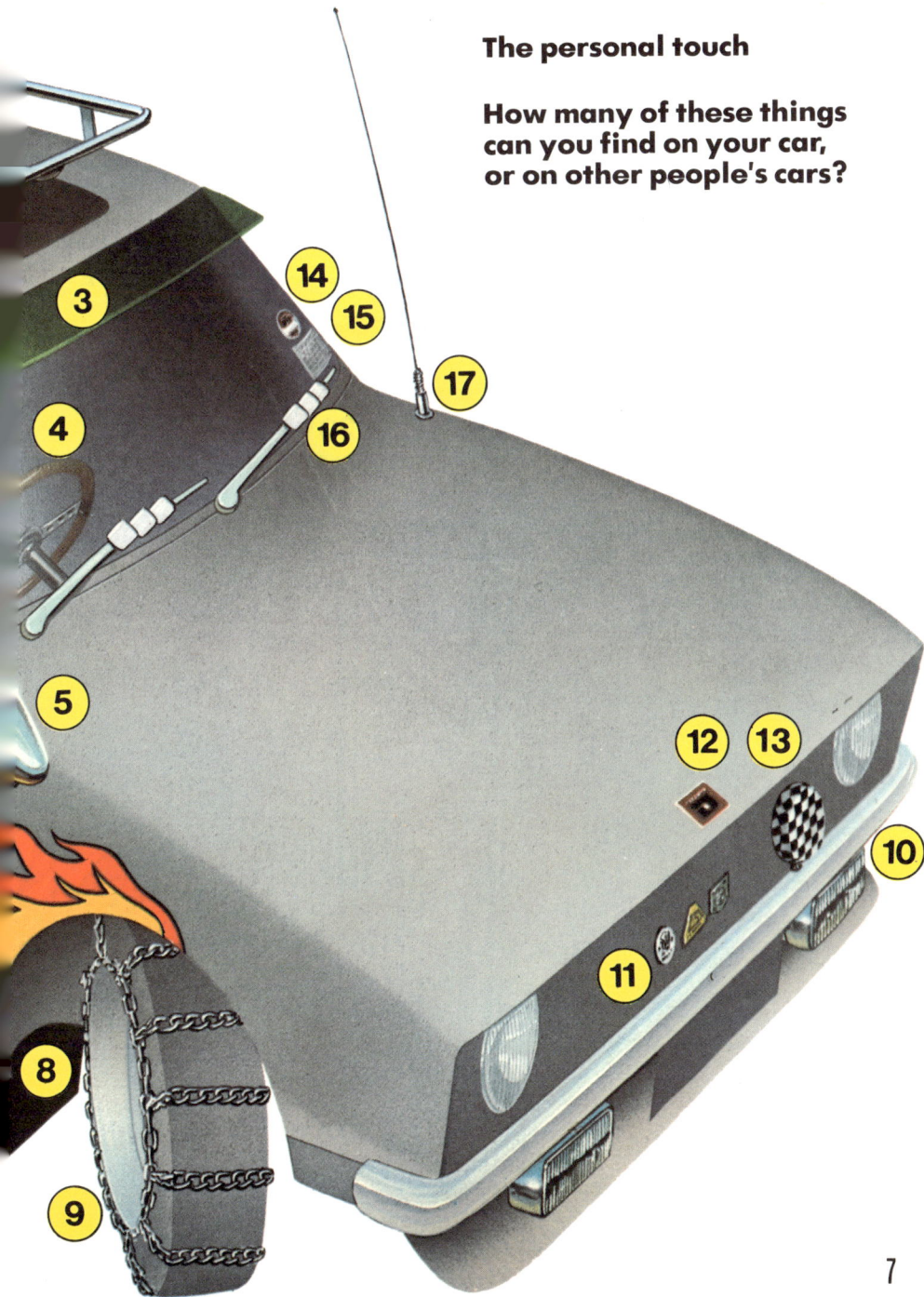

7

Motorway maze

Your car is about to run out of petrol.

8

Find the shortest route to the petrol station over or under the bridges — otherwise you'll be stuck!

1

Up in the sky

The sky is changing all the time. What is it like today?
Can you see an aircraft vapour trail or a rainbow?
Do you know the names of different kinds of clouds?

4

7

8

10

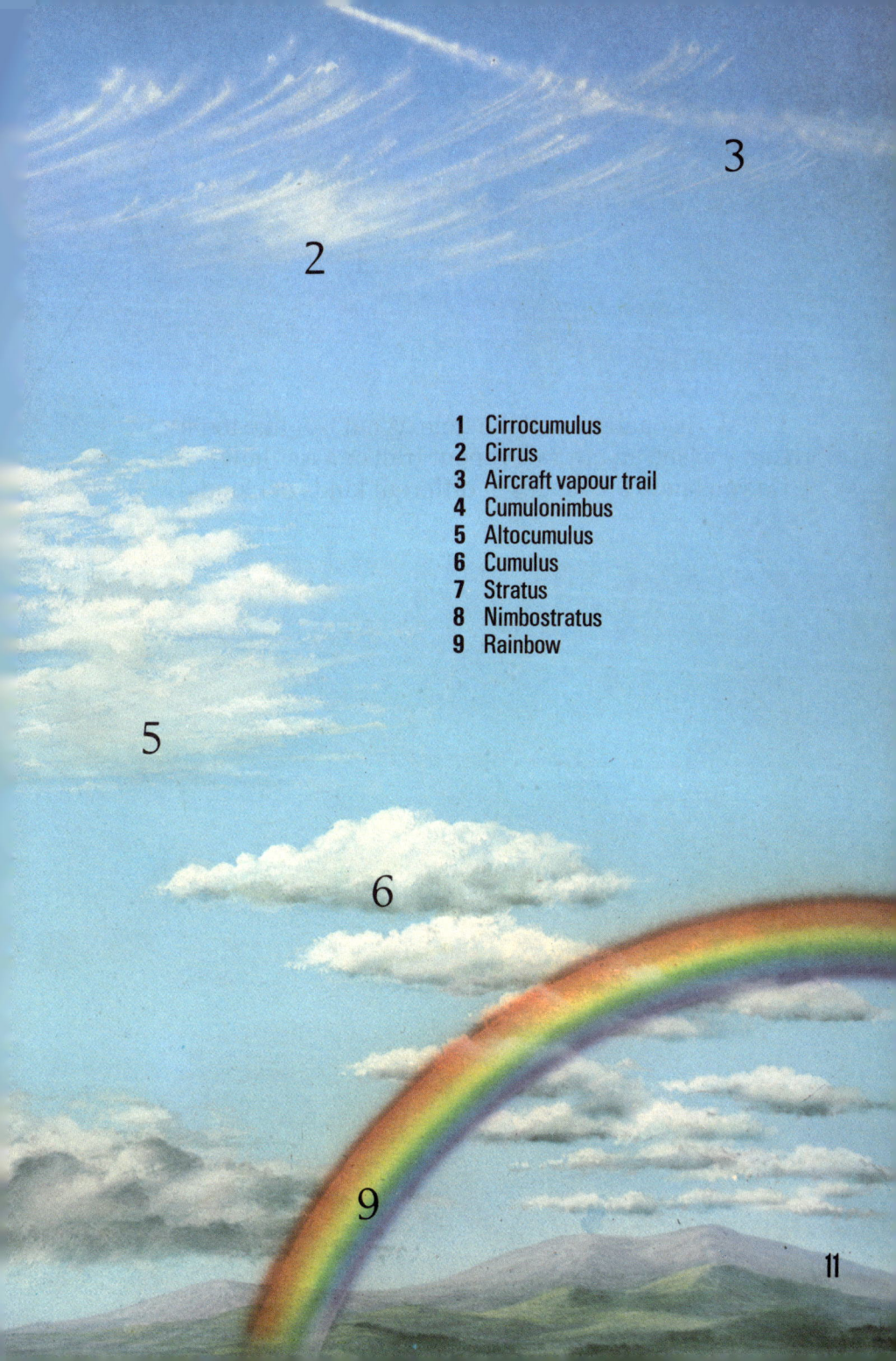

3

2

1 Cirrocumulus
2 Cirrus
3 Aircraft vapour trail
4 Cumulonimbus
5 Altocumulus
6 Cumulus
7 Stratus
8 Nimbostratus
9 Rainbow

5

6

9

11

Roadside animals

Have you ever seen any of these animals?
Where do you think each of them lives?

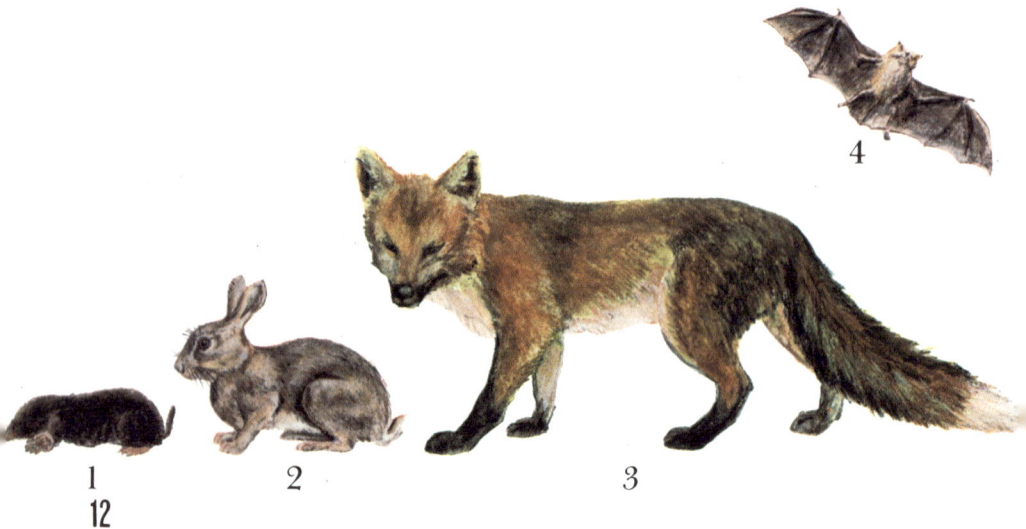

1

2

3

4

1 Mole lives in tunnels marked by molehills **a**
2 Rabbit lives in a warren under the ground **b**
3 Fox lives in other creatures' empty holes **c**
4 Bat sleeps in old buildings **d**
5 Badger lives in a set dug underground **e**
6 Hedgehog lives under dead leaves **f**
7 Squirrel lives in trees **g**
8 Fieldmouse lives in a nest in a cornfield **h**

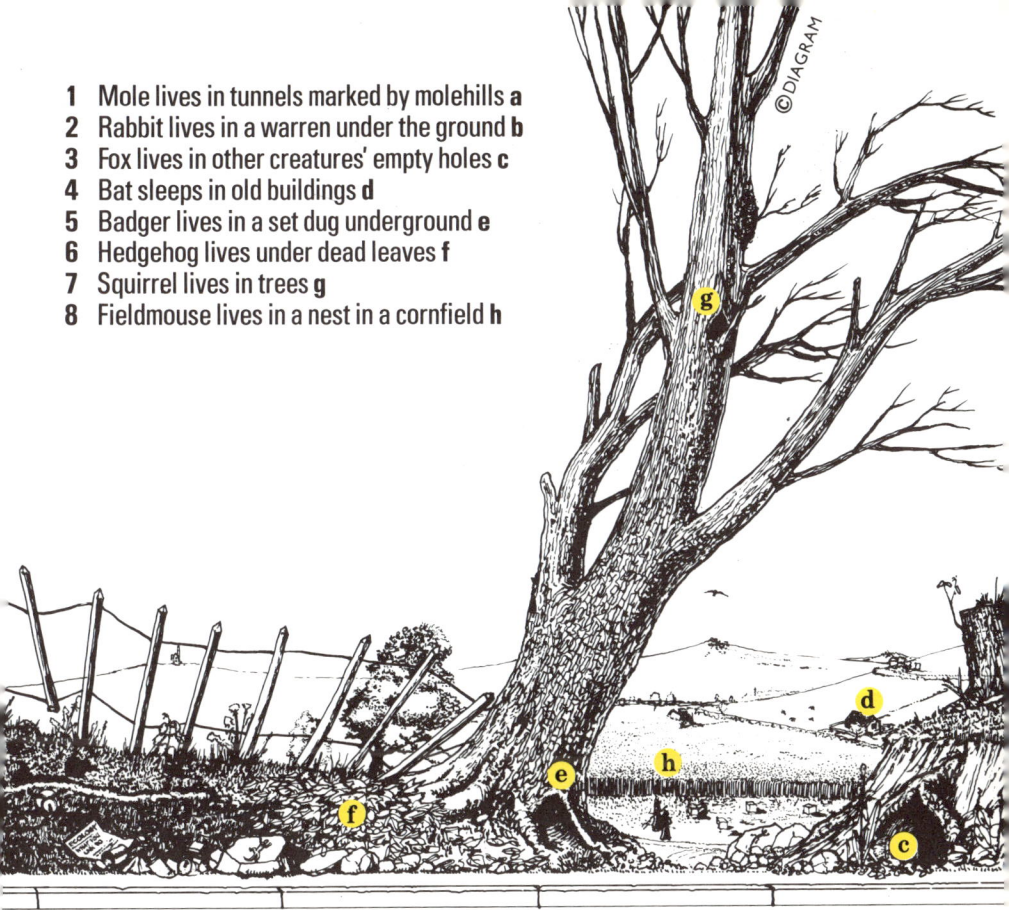

5

6

7   8

Signs to see   How many of these signs can you spot?

1

2

3

5
30

6
1 : 6

4

8

9
250 yds

7

10

1 No entry
2 Quayside or river bank
3 Keep left
4 No stopping
5 Minimum speed limit
6 Steep hill upwards
7 Beware wild animals
8 No through road
9 To public telephone
10 Turn left ahead
11 Markers approaching
    concealed level crossing
12 Uneven road
13 Parking
14 Road narrows on nearside
15 No left turn

Travelling by road

Can you sit these people from different

1 2 3 4 5

7 Mail coach

6 7 8 9

10 Horse bus   14 Early

10 11 12 13

6 Ambulan

14 15 16 17

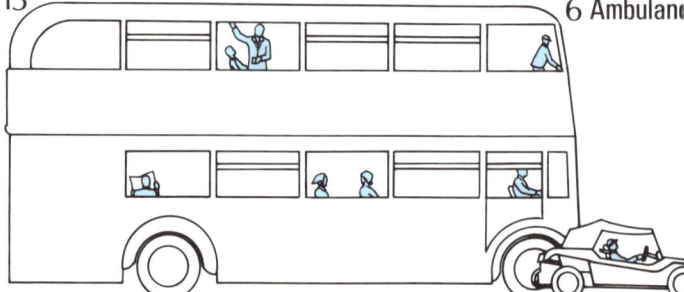

5 London bus   13 Beach bugg

16

times and places in their own vehicles?

3 Travois

8 Stage coach

2 Delivery van

16 Steam bus

4 Vintage car

11 Police car

1 Getaway car

17 Troop carrier

© DIAGRAM

15 Coach

12 Future car

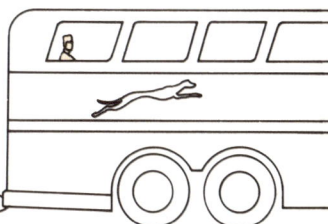

9 Greyhound bus

17

Special buildings

You can see many unusual buildings and structures on a journey. Here are the silhouettes of some of them. Do you know what they are?

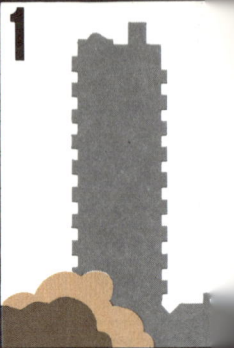

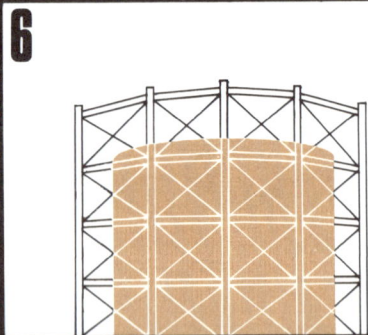

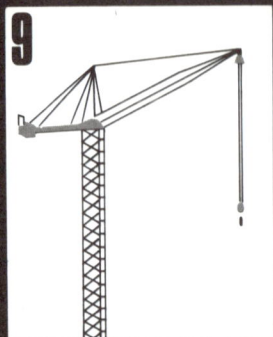

1

5

6

9

10

11

16

18

17

1 Block of flats	**8** Oast house	**13** War memorial
2 Power station	**9** Crane	**14** Television mast
3 Statue	**10** Lighthouse	**15** Windmill
4 Ancient stone circle	**11** Head of a coal mine	**16** Aerodrome
5 Cathedral	**12** Dutch barn	**17** Cooling tower
6 Gas cylinder		
7 Castle		

Know your manufacturer

Every firm that makes cars has its own emblem. Do any of these appear on your car? How many others can you find?

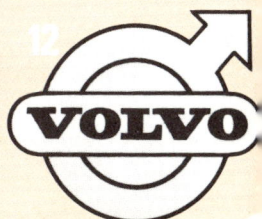

21

Naturalist's notebook

How many of these creatures can you see today? Here is a hint: many of them live on farms, some of them in homes too.

2

1

3

7

8

10

11

12

4

5

6

9

1	Cow
2	Deer
3	Swan
4	Horse
5	Goose
6	Goat
7	Pig
8	Sheep
9	Highland cow
10	Cat
11	Duck
12	Dog
13	Cockerel

13

Get to know a car's inside

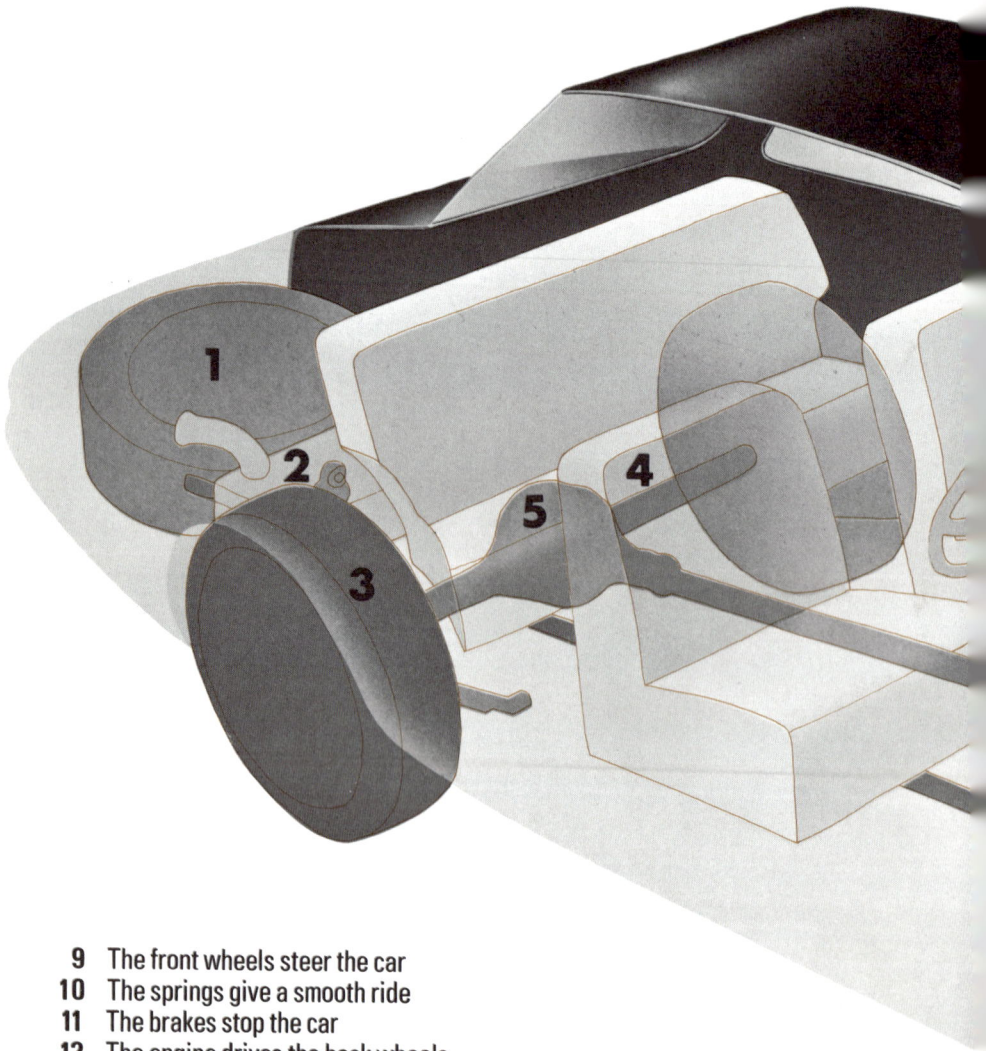

9   The front wheels steer the car
10   The springs give a smooth ride
11   The brakes stop the car
12   The engine drives the back wheels
13   The radiator keeps the engine cool
14   The clutch pedal helps to change gear
15   The brake pedal controls all the wheels
16   The accelerator pedal makes the engine go faster

These are some of the important parts of a car.

1 The spare wheel is in case of a puncture
2 The petrol tank holds the fuel
3 The back wheels drive the car along
4 The axle joins the rear wheels
5 The drive joins the axle to the engine
6 The steering wheel controls the front wheels
7 The brake lever controls the back wheel brakes
8 The gear shift changes the gear

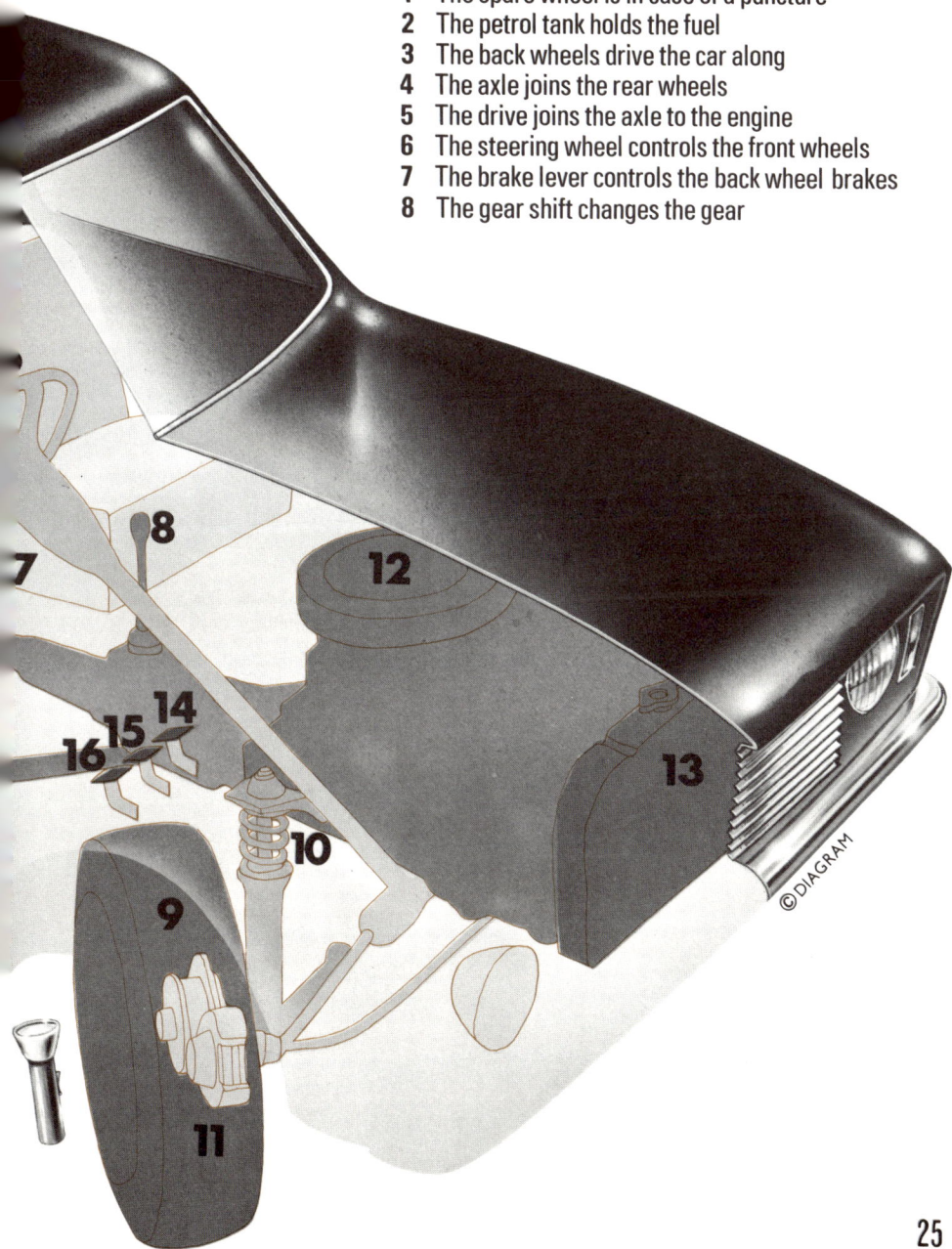

Rolling along

Which wheel fits which vehicle?

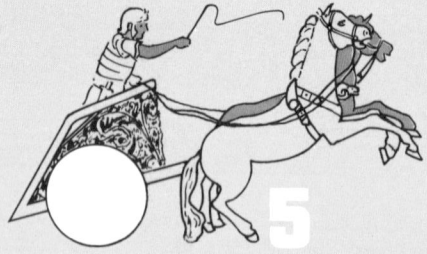

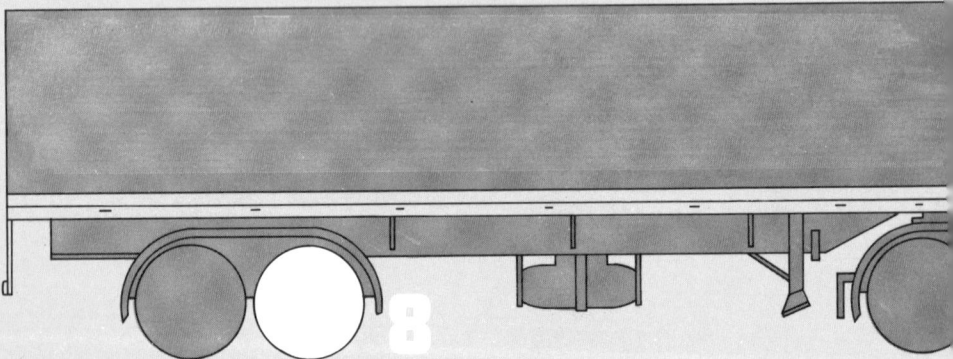

©DIAGRAM

1

4

5

8

d

a

c

f

e

b

h

26

1 Army troop carrier has wheel **a**
2 Penny-farthing bicycle has wheel **b**
3 Moon buggy has wheel **c**
4 Veteran car has wheel **d**
5 Chariot has wheel **e**

6 Early railway engine has wheel **f**
7 Ox-drawn cart has wheel **g**
8 Long distance American truck has wheel **h**
9 Road roller has wheel **i**

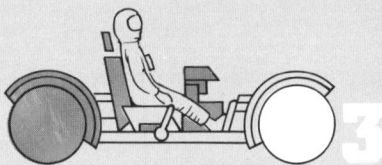

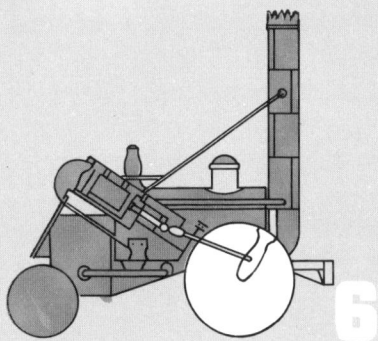

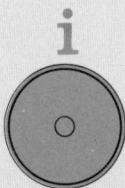

Strangers ahead

F

D

USA

GB

28

When it travels abroad, every motor vehicle must have a sign showing which country it comes from. Find out which nation these vehicles belong to.

©DIAGRAM

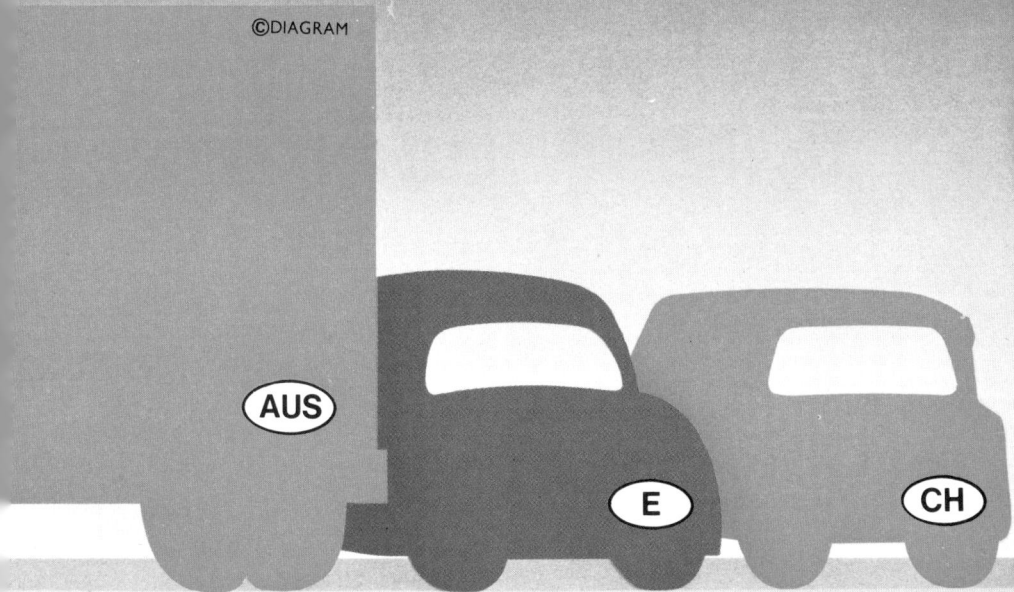

F	France	**USA**	United States of America
D	Germany	**GB**	Great Britain
DK	Denmark	**AUS**	Australia
S	Sweden	**E**	Spain
NL	Netherlands	**CH**	Switzerland

29

Joining a club

Motorists like joining clubs
and collecting badges.
How many of these badges
can you see?
Which are their clubs?

1 Automobilclub von Deutschland
2 Touring Club de France
3 Irish Motor Racing Club
4 Touring Club Italiano
5 Royal Automobile Club
6 Automobile Association
7 British Automobile Racing Club
8 Kooninklijke Nederlandsche Automobiel Club
9 Vintage Sports-car Club
10 American Automobile Association

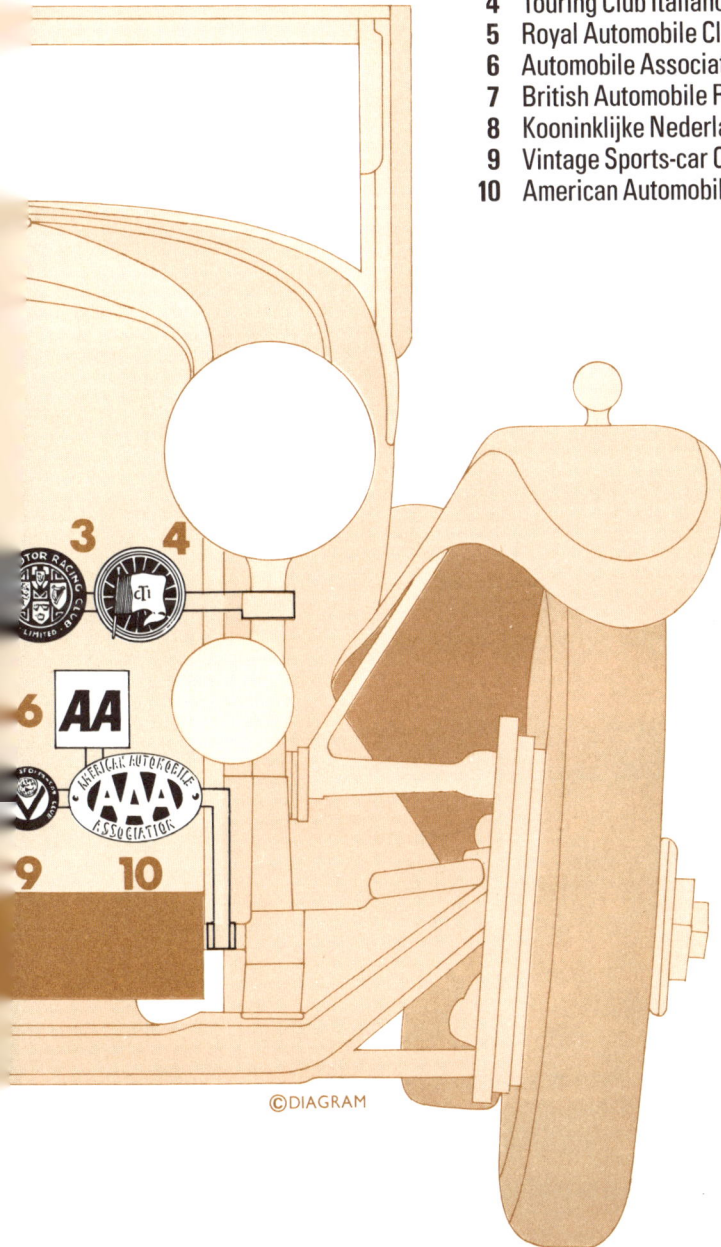

©DIAGRAM

Built for the job

Each of these vehicles does a special job.

Do you know what it is?

1 Road roller presses flat tarmac on the road
2 Shovel truck shifts earth or sand
3 Snow plough clears snow from the road
4 Fork-lift truck lifts crates and boxes
5 Crash truck pulls damaged vehicles
6 Racing car competes in races
7 Road sweeper cleans the road
8 Moon buggy takes astronauts over the moon's surface
9 Land Rover and trailer transport horses
10 Landing craft lands soldiers on beaches

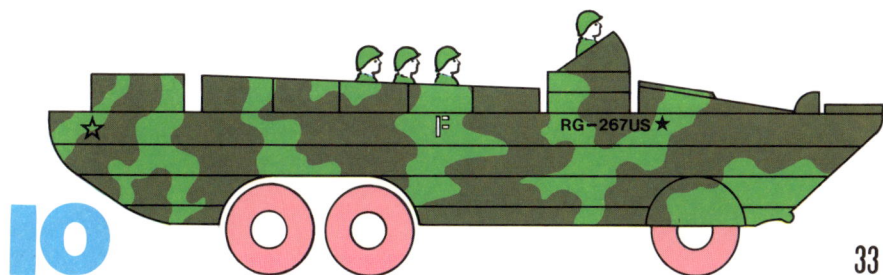

©DIAGRAM

RG–267US ★

Trees and leaves

Can you find any of the leaves shown at the bottom of the page?
Which trees are they from? Why not collect some of them
and press them in a scrap book?

1

2

3

e

b

d

©DIAGRAM

4   5   6

c

f

a

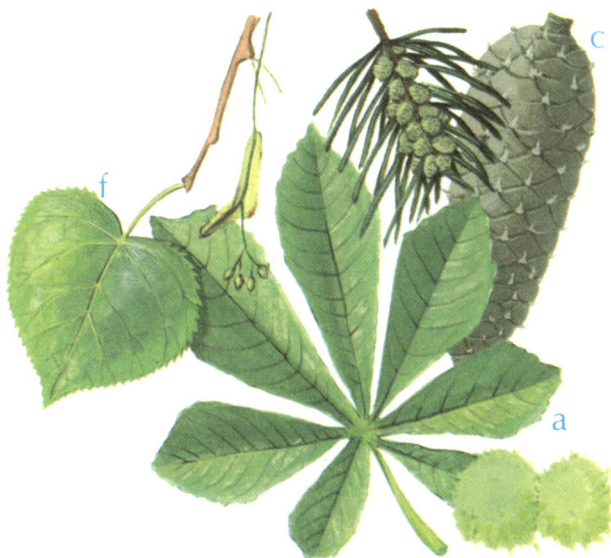

1 Horse-chestnut **a**
2 Sycamore **b**
3 Silver fir **c**
4 Ash **d**
5 Oak **e**
6 Lime **f**

Attention! Men at work
Have you ever seen anyone doing these jobs?

1 Hunting
2 Herding sheep
3 Repairing the road
4 Laying cables
5 Repairing telephone wires
6 Cleaning the road
7 Painting white lines
8 Laying paving stones
9 Surveying
10 Inspecting the drains
11 Cleaning lamps
12 Sweeping the streets
13 Helping children cross the road

©DIAGRAM

37

Plants

These plants often grow in banks and hedges along quiet country roads.
Find as many as you can — but be very careful to keep a look out for traffic.

1 Red poppy
2 Clover
3 Buttercup
4 Dandelion
5 Bluebell
6 Primrose
7 Cow parsley

1

2

3

4

5

7

©DIAGRAM

6

Unusual cargoes

All kinds of things — and creatures — are carried on roads. Can you fit each of the items at the bottom of the page to the correct carrier?

©DIAGRAM

40

3

1 Tank carries shells for its guns **a**
2 Transporter carries cars **b**
3 Circus lorry carries circus animals **c**
4 Heavy transporter carries tanks **d**
5 Refrigerated lorry carries meat **e**
6 Cattle truck carries farm animals **f**
7 Removal van carries furniture **g**
8 Timber lorry carries wood **h**
9 Dumper truck carries sand **i**

Birds

Have you ever seen any of these birds? Do you know their names? When you've spotted one of them, write down its name in your spotting book.

1

2

3

4

5

8

1 Peregrine falcon
2 Swallow
3 Wren
4 Teal
5 Barn owl
6 Herring gull
7 Raven
8 Heron

6

7

43

Bridges

Why do you think there are different types of bridges? How many have you been over?

1

2

3

4

5

6

44

©DIAGRAM

1 Steel arch bridge
2 Box girder bridge
3 Transporter bridge
4 Drawbridge
5 Suspension bridge
6 Arched beam bridge
7 Swing bridge
8 Lift bridge
9 Cantilever bridge

3

9

8

7

Try and work out how the bus can cross each bridge once only without going down the same road twice.

1

Small creatures

All around you, lots of small
creatures lead their lives.

How many have you ever found?

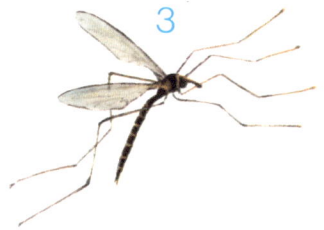

3

2

7

8

12

11

©DIAGRAM